SUMMARY OF PERMISSION TO FEEL:

Unlocking the Power of Emotions to Help Our Kids, Ourselves, and Our Society Thrive

By

Marc Brackett, PhD

BlinkRead

Copyright © 2020 by Blinkread.
ISBN: 9798668322565

All rights reserved.
This book or any portion thereof may not be reproduced or used in any manner whatsoever without the express written permission of the publisher except for the use of brief quotations in a book review.

Table of Content

SYNOPSIS 6

ABOUT THE AUTHOR 7

INTRODUCTION 8

LEARNING TO IDENTIFY AND ACCEPT HIS EMOTIONS TRANSFORMED THE AUTHOR'S LIFE. 10

EMOTIONS HELP US KNOW OURSELVES AND HOW TO NAVIGATE THE WORLD. 13

BEFRIENDING OUR NEGATIVE EMOTIONS WILL ALLOW US TO HARNESS THEM FOR POSITIVE OUTCOMES. 17

HUMANS AREN'T BORN WITH EMOTION SKILLS, BUT WE CAN ALL LEARN TO BECOME EMOTION SCIENTISTS. 21

THE RULER CURRICULUM ASKS US TO START GATHERING INFORMATION BY RECOGNIZING AND UNDERSTANDING EMOTIONS. 25

LABELING STRONG EMOTIONS WITH ACCURACY AND SPECIFICITY MAKES THEM LESS SCARY 29

EXPRESSING AND REGULATING OUR EMOTIONS WILL ALLOW US TO MANAGE SITUATIONS THAT TRIGGER US. 32

REGULATING OUR OWN EMOTIONS HELPS US TEACH OUR CHILDREN HOW TO DEAL WITH THEIRS 35

USING THE RULER CURRICULUM CAN CAUSE AN EMOTION REVOLUTION IN OUR SCHOOLS AND WORKPLACES. 38

SUMMARY KEYPOINT 42

BLINKREAD 44

DISCLAIMER:

This is a book summary of Permission to Feel Unlocking the Power of Emotions to Help Our Kids, Ourselves, and Our Society Thrive By Marc Brackett, PhD and is not the original book. This book is not meant to replace the original book but to serve as a companion to it.

SYNOPSIS:

Permission to Feel (2019) reveals that our emotions play a vital role in our cognitive processes, physical health, and relationships – but most of us don't know how to identify exactly what we're feeling, and why. Luckily, all of us can learn to be more emotionally intelligent by practicing emotion skills. This trains us to identify what we're feeling, understand where the emotion is coming from, and manage our triggers. By giving ourselves permission to truly experience all of our emotions, we can greatly reduce stress and increase our well-being.

ABOUT THE AUTHOR:

Marc Brackett, PhD, is a research psychologist, the founding director of the Yale Center for Emotional Intelligence, and a professor in the Child Study Center at Yale University. He is also the lead developer of RULER, a curriculum for developing emotional intelligence, which has been taught to over one million students of all ages across the globe.

INTRODUCTION.

Befriend your difficult emotions and learn how to harness them for good.

Have you ever had the experience of flying off the handle without knowing why? Do you often find yourself feeling exhausted or gloomy?

Emotions influence every aspect of our lives, from our relationships to our decision-making abilities. Yet even the most intelligent of us lack vital skills in recognizing and regulating our own emotions.

A lot of us have been taught to push our feelings away, making it difficult to express how we feel. We compulsively ask others how they're doing but don't connect long enough to listen or give an honest answer when asked the same question.

But suppressing our emotions has serious consequences. Our feelings become magnified and distorted, which can lead to chronic stress and depression, as well as negatively affect our physical health.

The good news is that all of us can learn how to identify – and deal with – our emotions. This makes them our allies instead of enemies, arming us with vital information about ourselves and the world.

In these blinks, you'll learn

How to become an emotion scientist;
How bad behavior can be a cry for help; and
Why emotional intelligence has been dismissed by scientists for so long.

Learning to identify and accept his emotions transformed the author's life.

As little kids, we freely express our emotions. But as we get older, many of us are told to toughen up and push those feelings away – with terrible results for our well-being.

The author, Professor Marc Brackett, is very familiar with that experience. As a young boy, he was in constant emotional pain. He was bullied at school and sexually abused by a neighbor who was a family friend. To make matters worse, his community socially ostracized him when the abuse was discovered.

Struggling with their own problems, his parents couldn't provide any support – his mother was an alcoholic, and his father was always enraged. They had no idea how to deal with their own emotions, let alone his.

The key message here is: Learning to identify and accept his emotions transformed the author's life.

Like generations before him, Marc learned to push his feelings down, hoping to make them disappear. He was so successful that he became completely numb.

But ignoring his emotions only made them stronger – and even more toxic. It affected his behavior. He did badly in school, fought with his parents, and was generally surly and misbehaved. Most people found him unpleasant and avoided him, or punished him. But nobody stopped to question why he was acting out. Until, in the author's own words, "a miracle took place." This miracle came in the form of his uncle Marvin.

Marvin was a teacher. Unlike other adults in Marc's life, he really took the time to listen. He showed Marc that he valued his company.

One day, he asked him a seemingly simple question: "How are you feeling?" No one had asked him that before – especially not someone who really wanted to know the answer. Suddenly, all of Marc's sadness, loneliness, and anger flooded out of him. He sobbed and released his feelings for the first time.

With this life-changing moment, the author opened a window to his feelings; now he could finally start learning how to deal with them. Despite being painful, releasing all those years of bottled-up emotions allowed him to start connecting with himself. Thus began his journey of healing and a career dedicated to helping others deal with their emotions.

Emotions help us know ourselves and how to navigate the world.

We often hear people talk about whether to follow their head – their rational reasoning – or their heart, which is their emotional reasoning. But this idea that emotions and thoughts aren't already connected is completely misguided. In fact, emotions affect every aspect of how we think. They shape how we make decisions, how well we can concentrate, and even what we think about.

The key message here is: Emotions help us know ourselves and how to navigate the world.

So why are we so convinced that emotional and cognitive processes have nothing to do with each other? Because that's what we've been taught for thousands of years. The Stoic philosophers of ancient Greece proclaimed that our emotions were not to be trusted. They believed emotions would distract from logical reasoning. Up until the 1980s, even psychologists treated emotions as if they were a distraction.

It was only in 1990 that the first research supporting emotions as a serious form of intelligence was published. Psychologists Peter Salovey and John Mayer formulated the first theory of "emotional intelligence." In their publication, they defined it as the ability to identify feelings and emotions in oneself and others, and to use this information to guide our behavior.

Since then, a rush of experiments by social scientists and psychologists have proved, beyond a doubt, that emotions are a key part of our cognitive processes.

In fact, our brains gather information from our senses to process a response to stimuli with a feeling. That feeling informs how we act, and even perceive, the world. That's what psychologists call a "cognitive loop." For example, when we're feeling happy, we're more likely to notice things around us that make us feel even better. We also spend more time pondering happy memories that can improve our mood. But the opposite occurs when we're feeling down: we're more likely to notice things that make us feel worse and ruminate on negative thoughts that weigh us, and our feelings, down.

Our mood also influences our decision-making. For example, feeling anxious may make us more cautious as we assume a negative outcome. On the other hand, feeling excited may make us overly optimistic and underestimate the risks.

There is no such thing as choosing with our heads or our hearts. They're already in cahoots, working together to help us process information and respond sensitively to the world.

Befriending our negative emotions will allow us to harness them for positive outcomes.

Who wants to feel depressed or irritable? No one! That's why we usually hide difficult emotions with a smile. But suppressing emotions can lead to chronic stress, which has disastrous consequences on our bodies.

Extreme stress keeps the body in survival mode, making it suspend longer-term "building and repair" projects that strengthen our bodies.

So how can we deal with negative emotions differently?

The key message here is: Befriending our negative emotions will allow us to harness them for positive outcomes.

Left unresolved, painful emotions can lead to chronic illnesses, like depression or anxiety. This unresolved pain is associated with unhealthy habits including poor diet, smoking, and lack of exercise. These factors, in turn, contribute to severe health issues like heart disease, cancer, and diabetes.

This chronic cycle happens because emotions cause our brains to release hormones and neurochemicals, which cause physiological reactions within our bodies. Intense outbursts of anger, for instance, can lead to heart disease. They flood our bodies with adrenaline and make our heart rates go up. With such dire consequences, it's no wonder we avoid negative emotions. But by allowing them to exist, they become useful tools.

For example, when doing a critical task like editing a job application, or making an important decision like buying a house, it's useful to have a healthy dose of fear. This short-term stress narrows our focus, allowing us to catch all the details. It brings out our inner perfectionist and keeps motivating us to work harder, do better, and consider all potential future risks. Completing the same application in a joyful, buoyant state might lead to an over-optimism that inadvertently minimizes risks and misses some important details.

Feeling angry can make us very uncomfortable, and most of us try to avoid it. But anger is one of the most useful emotions of all. It reveals our boundaries and underlines what's important to us. It also propels us into action, forcing us to confront what angers us.

If we suppress or ignore negative emotions, they get more intense and go from being useful to toxic. So instead of using anger to fix what's wrong around us, we use it to beat ourselves up. Or instead of using anxiety's fearful insights to make better decisions, we ignore it until we have a panic attack.

Valuing negative emotions allows them to work for us and not against us.

Humans aren't born with emotion skills, but we can all learn to become emotion scientists.

Say we want to get good at something like tennis or computer programming; we understand that those skills won't just come naturally. But it seems surprising that we actually have to practice what the author calls "emotion skills" to develop our emotional intelligence. After all, we've had feelings ever since the day we were born. Shouldn't we be experts by now?

Here's the thing. We aren't born with emotional intelligence. While some people may be naturally compassionate or sensitive, it doesn't necessarily mean they know how to navigate their own emotions. Also, emotional intelligence isn't linked to a person's IQ. In fact, people with high IQs often struggle with understanding their own, and other people's, emotions.

The key message here is: Humans aren't born with emotion skills, but we can all learn to become emotion scientists.

At its heart, emotional intelligence is about learning how to identify and manage our emotions. It's about giving ourselves permission to feel the good things and the bad. It's also about recognizing the role of emotions in social relationships – and supporting other people in managing their emotions too.

So, how do we do this? We need to become what the author calls "emotion scientists." As the name suggests, we should be willing to experiment and learn everything we can about emotions. Most importantly, this involves being open-minded.

We don't need to start thinking about whether an emotion is good or bad, productive or harmful. We simply need to identify it and learn to understand where it's coming from. And it's important to note that gaining emotion skills doesn't mean that we suddenly become perfectly zen. We may still fly off the handle or lash out at someone. But emotional intelligence helps us to recognize why that happens and learn how to manage the triggers better next time.

Luckily, emotional intelligence can be taught to adults and children in any classroom or workplace. Experiments with students at a business school showed that even just 16 hours of training greatly improved their skills at recognizing emotions.

To this end, the author has developed a syllabus consisting of five key skills, which anyone can learn. The acronym "RULER" stands for Recognizing, Understanding, Labeling, Expressing, and Regulating. The first three skills allow us to practice identifying our emotions. The last two allow us to develop the skills needed to deal with them.

Are you ready to begin your training? Let's dive in.

The RULER curriculum asks us to start gathering information by Recognizing and Understanding emotions.

Imagine your teenage child comes home from school furious and combative. She tells you that she hates you, she hates school, and she hates everything about her stupid, crummy life. Then she stomps upstairs and slams the door to her bedroom.

Her behavior is designed to push you away. She's practically begging for a fight. But if you give in and start shouting back, you'll miss a vital opportunity to find out what's actually going on. What's made your daughter feel so enraged? Where is this sudden hostility coming from? It may not seem like it, but her behavior is flagging an urgent cry for help.

This is where the "R" and "U" of the RULER curriculum come into play: it's so important to Recognize and Understand our emotions.

The key message here is: The RULER curriculum asks us to start gathering information by Recognizing and Understanding emotions.

In order to recognize emotions, we need to use all of our senses to gather information. What does the other person's facial expression tell us? Do they look relaxed or tense? Are their fists clenched? Do they sound strained? Are they speaking clearly and confidently, or are they mumbling?

These cues give us vital information, but they don't tell us everything. After all, we interpret expressions based on our cultural backgrounds, prejudices, and a host of other factors. In other words, we could be misinterpreting or projecting our own feelings onto the person.

That's why the author uses the mood meter to reduce misinterpretation when identifying emotions. Created by the psychologist James Russell, the mood meter is a graph that measures two key attributes of any mood: energy and pleasantness. This simple matrix gives us a way to categorize hundreds of moods into four key types. For example, you'll find anger and panic in the high energy and high unpleasantness quadrant. More depressed emotions are in the low energy and high unpleasantness quadrant.

The mood meter helps us identify emotions; next, we'll need to learn how to understand them. This skill requires us to explore one fundamental question: "Why?"

Why do you feel so angry? What triggered the feeling? Do you feel it often? Exploring these questions calls for a lot of gentle detective work and a very open mind. Rather than jumping to conclusions, we should allow ourselves to slowly inch our way toward a true answer.

Labeling strong emotions with accuracy and specificity makes them less scary.

What would happen if your Starbucks barista asked how you were doing, and you replied honestly? Imagine you told him that, actually, you're experiencing a sense of simmering anxiety and deep grief tinged with hopelessness?

The next time you went for your frappuccino, chances are he would smile nervously before scuttling away. The reality is, even though we ask people how they're doing, we don't really want to know. And our limited vocabulary for our own emotions makes it difficult to describe them beyond "Fine," "Busy," or just "OK."

Labeling our emotions with specific words is the next key skill in RULER that we need as emotion scientists.

The key message here is: Labeling strong emotions with accuracy and specificity makes them less scary.

As we've discussed, emotions are broadly categorized into one of the mood meter quadrants depending on their levels of energy and pleasantness. Now, let's dive into the specifics. If you're experiencing a high energy, very unpleasant feeling, it's important to pinpoint exactly what it is. Are you furious, or merely irritated? Are you terrified, or just a bit worried? These distinct shades of emotion have very different implications on how you feel.

Many of us fear labeling these strong feelings, for ourselves and others. It's as if speaking them aloud will make them more real. But the opposite is true – accurately labeling emotions is the first step to diffusing their murky powers.

An experiment at UCLA showed just that. Researchers placed participants with severe arachnophobia – a pathological fear of spiders – in the same room as spiders. One group had to describe the events in neutral language, and the other had to describe their feelings about it. The emotion-focused group was able to edge much closer to the caged spiders. Labeling their feelings made their phobia less powerful.

Articulating our emotions in clear language not only helps us make sense of them, but also allows us to get help. If other people understand what we're feeling, they may be more empathetic and willing to provide support. And the same goes with regard to our understanding of others.

At its essence, labeling emotions breaks through social isolation and allows us to connect with the world.

Expressing and Regulating our emotions will allow us to manage situations that trigger us.

Babies are screaming balls of emotion. Even without words, they let us know exactly what they need. If they weren't able to boldly demand food, warmth, and touch, they simply wouldn't survive.

But as we grow up our emotional needs become more complex – and so does our ability to express them. We may have language and a much larger vocabulary than a baby. But we also have the ability to hide our feelings.

That's why RULER reminds us to Express and Regulate our emotions.

The key message here is: Expressing and Regulating our emotions will allow us to manage situations that trigger us.

The author conducted a study with more than 5,000 school teachers, revealing that 70 percent of the emotions they felt were negative. But when asked in public, most of the teachers claimed to be happy most of the time.

Why would they hide their true feelings? Because of fear. We may think others will judge us or no longer want to be around us if they know the truth about our difficult emotions, so we say nothing at all. But, as the author experienced in his youth, repressing our emotions only compounds and intensifies them.

This makes learning how to express our emotions a crucial skill. Expressing is different than acting out or dumping our feelings on everyone around us because we're in a bad mood. It's about having the vulnerability to let other people in on the feelings underneath that bad mood.

All the skills we've learned so far have been preparing us for RULER's final step: Regulating our emotions.

We all have different triggers that make us feel strong emotions. Being able to anticipate these allows us to regulate our emotions better. For example, once we've identified a feeling, like experiencing isolation at parties, we can create strategies for dealing with that feeling when it comes up again. Another example of regulating emotions is the use of mindful breathing to feel less anger.

Regulating emotions is not about suppressing them. As we'll learn in the next blink, it's about fully accepting them and learning how to live with them in a productive way.

Regulating our own emotions helps us teach our children how to deal with theirs.

After teaching an emotion seminar for parents, the author was approached by a woman seeking advice. She was very worried about her son, who threw things out of anger and didn't regulate his emotions. She asked if she should take him to a psychologist. After providing a few strategies, the author was shocked to discover that the son was only eleven months old!

We often have wildly unrealistic expectations of how children should process emotions. When they're very young, children feel things with extreme intensity. But they have no control over what they're feeling, nor any way of regulating their emotions.

The key message here is: Regulating our own emotions helps us teach our children how to deal with theirs.

Before children can regulate their emotions by themselves, they must depend on an adult to provide coregulation. This can be as simple as hugging a child when they're distressed, or providing some distraction so they calm down during a tantrum.

As adults, we're behavior models for children, so it's important that we work on our own emotion skills. In addition to helping us teach our children, these skills grant us the insight needed for coregulation – especially if we're exhausted or enraged.

The first step is to identify the triggers that set you off at home. For example, do you get upset when you come home to a messy house? When you feel like that, it's important to take a few deep breaths to begin the regulation process. This helps you have a meta moment where you ask yourself, "How would my best self behave in this situation?" Also ask yourself, "Who is the parent I would really like to be?" Of course, you won't always be calm, loving, and nurturing. But taking a time-out to focus on that intention will go a long way toward embodying those characteristics.

Once you've identified your triggers, create strategies to anticipate them in the future. For example, if you always feel like exploding when you get home from work, use your commute to blow off some steam. Maybe it'll help to sing along to loud music, take a walk around the garden, or soak in a hot bath when you're feeling frazzled.

Teaching our children emotion skills by modeling them is teaching them a resilience that will serve them in every area of their lives.

Using the RULER curriculum can cause an emotion revolution in our schools and workplaces.

Imagine schools equipped with teachers who have the time and training to engage with their students. Or companies that are booming with motivated employees who feel safe to collaborate freely.

We know that emotion skills help us on a personal level and in the home. But that's just the start. Applying these skills in our schools and workplaces can transform how we learn, teach, and lead as a society.

The key message here is: Using the RULER curriculum can cause an emotion revolution in our schools and workplaces.

There isn't any other place where emotion skills are needed more than in our schools. Forty percent of American teachers leave the profession within five years. They report high levels of chronic stress, frustration, and feeling overwhelmed.

It's even worse for students. When the author surveyed 22,000 high school students from across the US, he discovered that 77 percent reported feeling tired, stressed, and bored. Is it any wonder that children find it difficult to learn?

Our modern workplaces are no better. The author's team conducted a survey of 16,000 American workers, posing questions like, "How do you feel at work?" Half of them reported commonly experiencing frustration and stress. Unsurprisingly, burnout is now widespread in many sectors.

The consequences of low emotional intelligence in workplaces and schools are very serious. But they can be mitigated if emotion skills are integrated on a structural level.

The author has taught the RULER curriculum in

thousands of schools. Students and teachers who proactively applied emotion skills in the classroom systemically saw dramatic improvements in stress levels and well-being.

With the same kind of commitment, RULER has achieved similar transformations in the workplace. Employees who feel engaged and inspired are more creative and productive. They're also much less likely to experience burnout. But they need the right emotional environment so they feel valued, appreciated, and free to speak openly about anything that bothers them.

Teaching emotion skills to managers can help create this safe environment. The author's research revealed that employees who had supervisors with strong emotion skills experienced around 50 percent higher happiness and inspiration – and 30 to 40 percent lower frustration, anger, and stress.

Emotionally intelligent schools and workplaces are places where creativity, learning, and innovation can thrive. This contributes not only to the well-being of those who study and work there, but to the success of the organizations overall.

SUMMARY KEYPOINT:

The key message in these blinks:

Emotions flood through our bodies all the time. They affect how we think and make decisions, how we relate to our children, and how we behave at school or work. By taking the time to develop our emotional intelligence, we build healthy relationships with our emotions. And this helps us become more motivated, empathetic, and resilient. Widely applied, these skills can cause an emotion revolution in our schools and workplaces, creating environments that nurture creativity, connectedness, and well-being.

Actionable advice:

Practice mindful breathing to calm your body and mind.

When you experience intense emotions, your body activates your stress response. This means your heart rate goes up, and your body is flooded with stress hormones. In order to calm this stress response, try practicing two minutes of mindful breathing. Sit somewhere comfortable, and close your eyes. Then breathe naturally through your nose for two minutes, focusing on your breath. Your heart rate will slow down, and you'll have more space to reflect on your emotions.

BLINKREAD

BlinkRead is dedicated to creating high-quality summaries of non-fiction books to help you through the bestseller list each week!

We cover books in self-help, business, personal development, science & technology, health & fitness, history, and memoir/biography. Our books are expertly written and professionally edited to provide top-notch content. We're here to help you decide which books to invest your time and money reading.

Absorb everything you need to know in 20 minutes or less!

We release new summaries each and every week, so join our mailing list to stay up-to-date and get free summaries right in your inbox!

Made in the USA
Coppell, TX
16 September 2021